No More

BONDAGE

To Bethany)
God bless you.

Bonita Onn

No More

BONDAGE

Breaking Free and staying free

BONITA QUINN

TATE PUBLISHING
AND ENTERPRISES, LLC

Published by Tate Publishing & Enterprises, LLC
127 E. Trade Center Terrace | Mustang, Oklahoma 73064 USA
1.888.361.9473 | www.tatepublishing.com

Tate Publishing is committed to excellence in the publishing industry. The company reflects the philosophy established by the founders, based on Psalm 68:11,
"The Lord gave the word and great was the company of those who published it."

Book design copyright © 2014 by Tate Publishing, LLC. All rights reserved.
Cover design by Jan Sunday Quilaquil
Interior design by Mary Jean Archival

Published in the United States of America

ISBN: 978-1-62994-594-1
1. Self-Help / Personal Growth / Happiness
2. Religion / Christian Life / Personal Growth
13.12.05

DEDICATION

To my wonderful husband, Charles, my knight in shining armor. To Drake and Whitney, my children. Thank you all for being who you are in my life. To my loving mother, Mrs. Lois Foster, for working hard and raising ten of us with love, fun, and protection.

ACKNOWLEDGMENTS

I thank God for guiding me through this process with grace and favor. I am deeply indebted to my dear friends, Karen and Phyllis, for making sure I meet deadlines and giving me so much of their time in assisting me. I truly do appreciate your willingness to help me do what God has entrusted me to do. You have graciously aided my journey throughout this book, and I am so blessed that God has sent you both in my life. May every person who turns each page experience true freedom through our loving Father.

CONTENTS

PREFACE

Decide today to break free.

I am truly amazed at what God has shown me, and I know he has given me a mandate to proclaim liberty to those who are bound. I believe that God desperately wants to show his people how to break free from all the bondage they find themselves in through the contents of these pages written under his influence. Christ set such a perfect example for us while here on earth that we need no other. I am convinced that his example of freedom from offense toward all who hated him is enough to keep us free as well. He does not want us bound by anything or any one. Bondage hinders us from completing the will of God in our lives, and it takes us away from really living the life that Jesus went through so much to give us. We each have custom-made lives given to us from God. I think that is so special. I have my own customized life that God has intended me to live, full of customized blessings along the way. Knowing his intent for us keeps us stable and aware of his true love for me.

Please allow the process of studying these pages and meditating on them to convince you of just how special you are to our loving Father. Trust what God has given me for you and allow him to captivate your thinking as he opens his heart up to you throughout this book. I do know freedom is a process for some, and it will take time to let what God has to say sink in to your mind, but believe me, it is worth every minute spent in the process.

As I skim through the pages of this book, I want to give you a sneak preview of what to expect throughout these pages. I begin with a description of my encounter with God that really gave me his objectives for this book. I had such a powerful encounter with God that he compelled me to get to the masses his heart concerning bondage. This is a very important matter to God, and he loves us so much that he is yelling through these pages to set my people free. I was so captivated by my encounter that I will never again take bondage lightly. As a matter of fact, I am acutely aware of bondage now, and I can sense it when I'm around someone in it. I then explain the types of bondage people find themselves experiencing, along with how to break free from bondage.

We will see how the King of kings set us free. We will study Stephen and how love kept Stephen free of offense. We study the life of Joseph and how his forgiveness is so much an example for us to remember and exemplify as we have so many different struggles throughout life. Finally, we describe what I call functioning bondage where people are living in bondage and are accustomed to it being a part of their lives.

INTRODUCTION

God's love is so abundant toward us, and he is compassionate about setting us free from whatever holds us back from that pure love he desires to lavish on us. I love life and believe we all should live it according to the purpose we were created to live it. I am convinced through the school of hard knocks and the leading of the Holy Spirit that our Savior is looking upon us and is making his care for us apparent as he continues to show us the life we are intended to live. We should be able to freely love without pretense and without condemnation. However, when we allow people, circumstances, and unforgiveness to block our freedom to love others and ourselves properly, it takes so much of life from us. We become heavy, fickle, unstable, callous, and hard to get along with. When we are bound to anything holding us captive, we condescend to a low level of living that Jesus never intended for us to live. Jesus has demonstrated his deep concern and care for us over and over again throughout Scripture. As I meditate in his Word, I am more and more saturated with the confidence to live life free of all the damages that come along with living. I've learned that I don't have to just accept things in my life and live with them if they are not according to the Word. He has told me to pursue excellence and not settle for mediocrity.

The attitude I take toward life now is to live in full assurance of his love and acceptance toward me and who I have been created to be. I love me now and that took so much ministry from Christ. He pursued me because he knew how damaged I was, and now, I'm writing this to you as an extension of his message to you to break free and stay free as well. Even though bad things still happen to me, those things have nothing in me to hold on to any longer. I can get my emotions in check, although hard sometimes, and keep on trucking. I know how imperative it is to move forward in life without delay.

Destiny awaits, and I want everything in me to be used by God to help everyone I come in contact with in life. I also pray that this book reaches masses and masses of people and touch their hearts for a lifelong change that gives them the freedom to live without being bound any longer. I believe this book is meant to get you to recognize bondage and resist it at the onset. Not to be paranoid, but to be aware of what it is and what it does to you. I believe freedom has helped me to step out on faith. I believe freedom gives me exclusive rights to all God intended my life to become. I believe freedom is what it takes to live and love God's way. Why would Jesus go through what he went through to set us free if it were not crucial to life? God wants to make sure you get what his grace is willing to give us. He sent his grace to help us through our mistakes so we can get back up and move forward. Being stagnant literally frustrates the grace of God. Being bound frustrates the grace of God.

God desires to make our dreams come true. He wants to literally surpass what we expect. His unfailing love will never let us down. We can trust him with our deepest desires. We can also trust him with our deepest failures and past hurts, so they won't hinder our deepest desires. Those things won't get in the way of the free life. Those things won't be used by the enemy to let life pass us by while we are under the subjection of them. Life will be free of stuck places. We will learn from every mistake and live without regret because we have a compassionate heart and loving Father that forgives us and wants us to forgive. Please take the time to examine these pages and get what God has in store for you. I promise you, you won't regret it. You will be praising God that he cares so deeply for you and that he's coming to your rescue. Yes, I'm excited for you to join the many others of us that broke free and are loving it.

NO MORE BONDAGE

The Spirit of the Lord God is upon me because the Lord has anointed and qualified me to preach the Gospel of good tidings to the meek, the poor, and afflicted. He has sent me to bind up and heal the brokenhearted, to proclaim "liberty to the [physical and spiritual] captives, and opening of the prison and of the eyes to those who are bound" (Isaiah 61:1).

I woke up one night with the feeling of something tight around both of my wrists. I heard the Lord say, "My people are in bondage." I replied, "Yes, I know, Lord." I then proceeded to try and go back to sleep. I heard his voice again utter the same words, but with more emphasis. The tightness around my wrists felt tighter, and I could not ignore it any longer, I tossed and turned in the bed, trying to get what he told me out of my head and go back to sleep. It did not go away, but got worse to the point I literally began to feel what it felt like to be in bondage. I could not shake the feeling of despair and anguish. It was a troubling and helpless feeling that was so strong that I felt literal hurt in my heart for the people in bondage so much so that it brought tears to my eyes. I began to sob and cry out to God. My husband woke up and asked me what was wrong, and without thinking, I replied, "Bondage, so many people in bondage. God said, 'My people are in bondage to so many things, and they do not know how to get out. They are hurting and they feel helpless and stuck.'" My husband looked at me and said, "Oh." Then he rolled over and went back to sleep, snoring and all. I wanted so bad to share what I felt so he could possibly understand and somehow feel what I felt, but God was not talking to him, he was talking to me.

The bands around my wrists got tighter and tighter to the point that they started to hurt. Realizing that I could not just lie there and ignore it, I got up and went to another room and began to pray. I remember thinking that I could pray until the bands were loosened and my wrists would be free. I began to pray in my heavenly language, and it seemed like the more I prayed, the tighter my wrists felt. God then began to give me more and more of a vivid picture of what his people were going through. It made me feel terrible inside. I asked the Lord what is this bondage, and why did I feel so terrible? I was literally crying and sobbing with hurt and pain. It was a very bad feeling, and I am trying to put what I felt into words as best I can, yet I still have not captured the true essence of what I felt that night. I continued to pray and ask God until I heard him say that he hears the cries of the people and he wants to set them free. The Word of God says in John 8:36, "So if the Son liberates you [makes you free men], then you are really unquestionably free."

I began to think about the people of Israel when they were in bondage to Pharaoh. In Exodus 6:1, God told Moses, "Now you shall see what I will do to Pharaoh; for under compulsion he shall let them go, and under compulsion he shall drive them out of his land." What God was saying is that he was going to make it so obvious to Pharaoh that he was God and he wanted his people free and that Pharaoh would be the one to drive them out himself, instead of trying to keep them enslaved any longer in his land. God proceeded to tell Moses that he appeared to Abraham, Isaac, and Jacob as God Almighty, but by his name "Lord" or Yahweh or resident owner, he had not made known to them yet. God was saying to Moses that those were his people and no man will enslave them because "I am their God and beside Me, there is no other." God heard the groaning of the people of Israel as the Egyptians were holding them in bondage. God hears you too, even though you may not be saying a word, and he wants to free you. God's word says that he is touched with the feelings of our infirmities. He felt their pain and anguish, and he was going to use Moses to set them free. I felt God telling me as he told Moses to use this book as an instrument to allow him to set his people free today from the bondage they have found themselves under. I say *under* because the word *bondage* means "slavery, to be brought under." The people of Israel were under the burdens of what Pharaoh told them to do. The burdens that made them feel so hopeless and helpless, the burdens that took away their true character, the bondage that stripped them of their creativity, and the bondage that kept them down for so many years. God wants to free his people today from those same hopeless feelings of despondency. God wants you to know that he is God and he cares very deeply for you and he will see to it that you are set free. You don't have to walk around in anguish any longer. It's time to break free of all bondage in your life. Your freedom was purchased with the blood of Jesus, and because of his blood, you can be free today.

I will be focusing on the three kinds of bondage that the Lord has given me that is most prevalent in the lives of people today. The first one is being in bondage to another person/relationship. Second is bondage to circumstances, i.e., cares of life, burdens, drugs, alcohol, or issues in general. The third is bondage to yourself with the imprisonment of unforgiveness, resentment, and bitterness holding you hostage. I declare that these things will no longer hold you hostage, rule over you, and steal the blessed life God has in store for you. It is time to break free. I declare your freedom today in the name of Jesus.

BONDAGE TO ANOTHER PERSON/RELATIONSHIP

But I say, walk and live [habitually] in the [Holy] Spirit [responsive to and controlled and guided by the Spirit]; then you will certainly not gratify the cravings and desires of the flesh (of human nature without God). For the desires of the flesh are opposed to the [Holy] Spirit, and the [desires of the] Spirit are opposed to the flesh (godless human nature); for these are antagonistic to each other], so that you are not free, but are prevented from doing what you desire to do.

Romans 8: 4, 14–15 (AMP)

There are people who will not move unless someone else is okay with what they are going to do or telling them what to do. This is hard to admit, I know, but just sit back and analyze yourself and see if this remotely resembles you. If so, freedom is near. You were never meant to be controlled by anyone. Neither were you meant to control anyone else. Either condition yields misery. Many times the act of controlling another comes from being hurt in the past, and fear of being hurt again, which is a defense mechanism. The person being controlled is in bondage, and the person doing the controlling is also in bondage. Break free! Don't settle for bondage!

Many people are being held down by someone else's opinion. How they feel or think things should be and you know in your heart that God is telling you otherwise. First, you have to see it as bondage. Then you have to go to God and tell him you have a real problem with it, and then you will start to see him move on your behalf. He will start to shake the relationship up and use circumstances to keep you apart and allow you to act on your own free will, not apart from him, but apart from them. The author and finisher of our faith is readily available to free you from such bondage. Trust God and let God be God in your life. The relationship could very well be a blessing, but be careful not to put the blessing over the Blesser, God himself. Under no circumstances should anyone be put above God. Check yourself on this. When something happens, do you think of what God would say? Does scripture come to mind or do you think of what that person would think or say? Do you call that person before calling on God about it, or do you simply call that person and pray about it later, knowing you will do what that person said and not wait on an answer from God? We must understand that God is the only true God, but when you allow someone else's opinion to be above what God is telling you to do, you have just given them the ability to be God in your life. It is so easy to fall into this particular trap that you don't even know you are there unless God starts to show you. Now I'm not talking about a friendship that you share with someone that is a healthy relationship or spouse. You can tell if that relationship is in its proper place. He does not want to destroy the relationship, but what he does want is to be first in our lives so that he can lead and guide us into all truth about whatever is going on in our lives. He is there for us to be our security and fortress. God knows better than any other human, whats best for us. He wants us to prosper and be in good health, to include having healthy relationships.

When I felt the tightness as if I had on handcuffs around my wrists, I felt my right wrist being held tighter than my left one. It was so tight, and it was also pulling me down to the point that I was slouched over slightly on the couch. My right wrist was aching, and I wanted it to go away. Oh, it was miserable. God said, "That's how bondage feels when you want to get out and you think you can't." He said one of your wrists feels more bound than the other because a part of them wants to be free and can really see that freedom, but a part of them is being held captive by the enemy to keep them from what I truly have for them. Freedom is attainable, but you have to step out on faith to receive it.

The intensity in my wrists got even tighter. I felt such strong feelings of heaviness and helplessness inside. He said, "I need for you to feel literally what it's like to be held down in bondage, so you can empathize and understand that it's not as easy to get free as you may think. Without my help, without faith, and without stepping out, they will never break free." I now long to help people get free.

Bondage is real, and it will kill self-esteem, freedom to live, and your livelihood. Bondage is tight. It makes you feel lifeless, hopeless, and stuck. It holds you down like you are being sat on. It's extremely heavy and debilitating. How can you feel and see yourself being held down by someone and not do anything about it. That is the enemy making you feel like you cannot do anything about your present circumstances. It's all a lie and a façade brought on by the enemy. He toys with your feelings. That's why it's important to realize we do not live by our feelings. Feelings are fickle. They are up and down according on the circumstances. We have to get a grip on our feelings or else, they will grip us and tell us what to think and do. We have to live by the word of God. God tells us what we should do through his word, not someone else's opinion. There is a spirit of heaviness that is cast upon a person in bondage.

Galatians 5:1 says, "It was for freedom that Christ set us free; therefore keep standing firm and do not be subject again to a yoke of slavery." God never intended for us to be enslaved to anything or anyone. Get free by trusting in him and not in man. Jesus died and rose again for our freedom. He has afforded us the opportunity to be free from all forms of bondage. Sometimes, people can see themselves held down, but because of a comfort zone they have created, they would rather stay bound and miserable. Who would want to live miserably? I'll tell you who: those who are afraid and without faith. The Holy Spirit is telling them to break free, but they continue to disobey and remain bound. Moaning and groaning on the inside, but yet bound and will not step out on faith and believe God will help them. There are those who are agitated and have no peace. Some are completely confused because they pray and God is saying, "Just claim your freedom, you can do all things through Christ." Then He will lead you to scriptures to stand on in the process.

I remember being in bondage to what people thought of me to the point that I started losing my hair. I literally had gaps in my head from hair loss. I had to go to the doctor to get shots of medication. I was consumed with their thoughts of me stepping out on faith to serve the Lord. I was so engulfed with their opinion of me that I did not even consider how it was holding up my destiny, my God-given destiny. Wow, think of that. I was so consumed with pleasing them that I did not realize they were standing between me and my true purpose and destiny. After looking back, I wish I had not given them so much power over me that I would be willing to jeopardize my future, my God-given destiny for them. You may say that's taking it a bit far, but not really when you think of your ideas and endeavors being held back by someone else's opinion. One endeavor can change your whole life and turn it around and point you in the right direction for purpose and destiny. Destiny is not a job, it's what you were created to do and be.

After making the decision to serve God with my whole heart, I went through much persecution from them. I was ostracized, minimized, and criticized, but God stepped right in and kept me through it all. He comforted me through the pain, but most of all, he began to cultivate me and show who he was to me and I was truly blessed to learn how to hear his voice and spend beautiful moments with him. He truly became Abba to me. The intimacy changed me forever. As He began calling me to his presence. I would wake up to a still small voice speaking to me and calling me, saying, "Bonita, my love, come." Even though I had so much growing to do and so much to learn, he wasn't really concerned with that. He just wanted to spend time with me and show me who I was. He told me how he wanted to teach me his word.

He blessed my family above and beyond anything I could ask or think. I began to depend on God more and more. The pain and heartache eventually went away. My relationship with him grew stronger and closer. I was so secure in knowing him that those feelings of hurt and pain that I felt while

you how real he is. There is a place in his presence that only he can take you, and there is a place in you that only he can go.

Some people do not know they are bound because they are so naive and trusting in man that they cannot see the bondage. It's one thing to be bound and not know it, it's entirely different to see yourself bound and feel so captivated by a relationship or a spirit that you cannot make a move without their approval. That is a python spirit that comes to choke the life out of you. In either case, you need the help of God to come between what separates you from freedom. The freedom he purchased with the blood of his dear son, Jesus Christ.

Ask yourself what price would anyone pay for you that would compare to the death on the cross. How about the suffering on the way to the cross? What about the persecution while he was here on earth? Who would go through so much suffering for us, but the lover of our souls. The Creator of the universe did it just for you and me. I don't know about you, but that is so special to me. I can only imagine the pain he went through to purchase our freedom. Sure, we read about it. There are even movies about it. He literally went through it. It was no small thing what they did to him. Yet he took it all for us. He knew what he was going to have to endure and just knowing about it made him so highly stressed that prior to his ultimate suffering on the cross he sweat great drops of blood when he was in the garden of Gethsemane. A condition called hematidrosis, which occurs when a person is suffering extreme levels of stress. "And being in agony, He prayed more earnestly. Then His sweat became like great drops of blood falling down to the ground" (Luke 22:44). Stop here and meditate on that scene so that he can show you a vivid picture of what he must have been going through. This is important for you to understand fully. Really take some time to meditate on it all, keeping in mind he did it for you.

BONDAGE TO CIRCUMSTANCES/THINGS

Arise [from the depression and prostration in which circumstances have kept you—rise to a new life]! Shine (be radiant with the glory of the Lord), for your light has come, and the glory of the Lord has risen upon you!

Isaiah 60:1

Life itself with all the ups and down and ins and outs can be heavy and burdensome. We find ourselves in things that if we had known going into them what price we would have to pay, we probably would not even attempt to endeavor to do them. We have so much going on that it all becomes so heavy at times that it's hard to bear. The bills, the family issues, the job, and etc. are contributing factors to the bondage of circumstances. Then there are people who are dealing with addictions to cope with life issues. Being in bondage to drugs, alcohol, the cares of life will begin to control your way of thinking. These things weigh heavy on us and make us feel like there is no way out from under the debt, past mistakes, and all the things happening that the enemy has set up in our lives to make us feel bound by them. When life becomes overwhelming and you do not have anyone to go to for help, you start to take on all that you have to deal with, and these things are weighing heavy on your shoulders. Life and all that goes on in it does not overwhelm God. I am reminded of someone that has so much potential, but with all the burdens, they cannot even start to see what they have inside because they are stuck under circumstances that won't allow them to truly grasp what is at their disposal through the power of God to break through and open their eyes to see what they are really put here on earth to do. We were not put here to worry and be held down by what we have to deal with; quite to the contrary, we were put here to have dominion over all circumstances and issues in life by allowing God to use us to show his power over the enemy and what he tries to do in our lives and the lives of others. We were put here to help mankind and lead them to righteousness. We are God's chosen people, and he wants to use us and not allow circumstances to use us to show that there is nothing too hard for God. There is nothing impossible with God. God can handle all we have if we would just trust him and give it all to him. Yes, even our past mistakes. Those things we have done to bring things on ourselves. Yes, he especially wants to administer his grace to deal with those things because where sin abounds, grace much more abounds. God never expected us to be perfect in our behavior, but to allow him to show us how to behave and depend totally on him to lead us and guide us as we live this life. He expects us to be perfect as in complete in him.

Sometimes, we try so hard at being what others expect of us that we neglect what God expects of us. We start to put people in the place of God and try to please them instead of God. God wants to be the only true and living God in our lives. He wants to show himself strong in our lives to the point that we experience him in such a way that our confidence is built up in him and his love for us. When things happen, do you think, "Oh no, something else I have to deal with"? No, let's change that and think, "Oh well, something else God will deal with." Continue on in him and depend totally on what he says. How do you get familiar with his voice and the ways he communicates with us? I'm glad you asked. You do that by spending time with him. You do it by meditating on his word. Joshua 1:8 says, "This book of the law shall not depart from your mouth, but you shall meditate on it day and night, so that you may be careful to do according to all that is written in it; for then you will make your way prosperous, and then you will have success." When we meditate on the word, it becomes a part of us and our daily thought life begins to change, and as our thoughts change, our words change, when our words change, our lives changes. My life changed when I started meditating on the word. The word of God gave me such confidence in the love God has for me. I'm sure of His promises now and that they pertain to me and He will do what it takes to work on my behalf as I stay in Him. I began to speak his word daily over my life, and as his word began coming out of my mouth, they echoed back to me over and over again. I quickly changed all negative words that I spoke as I began to line up my thoughts and understand that I have to continue to bring them into the obedience of Christ and believe what He says, not what my circumstances were displaying to me. I realized my help came from the Maker of heaven and earth. It doesn't get any better than that. There is no one on earth smarter, do you agree? When I began to wait on God and experience him, I could sleep better. I could praise God better. God told me that as I praise him "through" my circumstances, I'm showing him that I trust him "with" my circumstances. I had to truly be conscious of my thoughts. My thoughts changed to God's perspective because I brought them into correct alignment with the Word of God.

"He will give you a spirit of praise instead of the spirit of heaviness" (Isaiah 61:3b). I did not worry so much. I used to be such a worrier. My thought life was out of control, and I expected negative things to happen to me. In Proverbs 15:15

it says, "All the day of the desponding and afflicted are made evil [by anxious thoughts and forbodings], but he who has a glad heart had a continual feast [regardless of circumstances]. You can literally think yourself into bondage. I know because I was in bondage to wrong thinking for years until I was introduced to the One that freed me from all sorts of bondage. I realized that most of my life had been made miserable by evil thoughts and forebodings. Even when things were great, I was miserable because my thoughts were poisoning my outlook and robbing me of enjoying life. I knew the word of God in Proverbs 23:7a, "For as he thinks in his heart, so is he." Knowing it was not good enough; I had to get in his word and meditate my way into believing what it says.

People say they have favorite scriptures and I have to admit there are some that come to mind more than others, but I often tell people my favorite scripture changes depending on what I am going through at the time. Whatever scripture God uses for me to speak and meditate upon for what I am going through becomes my favorite one at that time. It's funny, but true. I do have some that I quote on a daily basis because I daily want to believe them, but for the most part, my favorite one is the one that God uses to deliver me at that particular time. I don't want to hear healing scriptures when I have financial issues. You know what I mean? I give God the circumstance, he shows me the scripture to stand on, and that becomes the best one for me at that time. We must believe what the word says about what we are going through. We cannot believe his word if we do not begin to meditate on it so he can convince us of its truth in our spirits. The word of God has to connect with our spirit man in order for us to truly believe enough to step out on it, because if it's just head knowledge, we will not step out. The word of God has to penetrate through our very being and reach our spirit and that's where belief begins. I believe, I believe, I believe.

Some things I do right now, I can't explain other than my spirit leads me, and the next thing I know, I'm doing what the will of the Lord has told me to do. No, I don't mean that happens all the time and I go around spontaneously doing things, but I have to say that it does happen from time to time and the only explanation is God. Our spirit longs to commune with God. Our spirit is quickened by his leading. Through prayer and meditation, some things I know I can't explain how I know, I just know. That can only come from God. I can do nothing without him, but with him, I can do all things. If we merely listen to man, we will be so confused. Let those negative things man says about you go in one ear and out the other, nonstop. The word says he rewards those who diligently seek him. He rewards us with all the answers we need to get us through all the tough circumstances that life has to offer. Life hits hard sometimes and God knows how to play hardball with the best of them. Just step out of the way so that he can catch all your hardballs and deal with them.

When we try to catch those hardballs ourselves, they become too hard, too heavy, and too much. Remember, there is nothing too hard for God. There is nothing to complicated or terrible or shameful that God cannot fix. He wants to take away the burdens and give us rest and lightheartedness so that we can live in true freedom. He wants to give us joy unspeakable and full of glory. True freedom is a state of rest, peace, and contentment. "Godliness with contentment is great gain" (1 Tim. 6:6). True trust equals true freedom. When you trust in God, everything and everyone else is subject to what he says about them. He has the last say-so. He should be in the center of everything you do. Allow the leading of the Holy Spirit to reveal his will to you and lead you throughout life.

My husband and I have gotten to the point where we know God is for us and nothing can by any means harm us. God is our refuge, our fortress, our shield, and our buckler. We are kept in a place in God that the enemy is always defeated when he attacks. We rest in that truth no matter what is going on. "For in Him we live and move and have our being" (Acts 17:28a). God provides us with the right armor for each attack. He upholds us when we get weak and girds us up. His strength is made perfect in our weakness. We do not mind, neither are we too proud to say, "Lord, I'm weak, I need you." The Lord always shows up as our very present help each time we call. That is an absolute fact.

I'm reminded of the time my daughter was a victim of attempted rape. It was an extremely hard time in our lives. Our precious thirteen–year-old was a victim of that terrible injustice. It took so much from her. She was never the same after that. She held on to it for a year before she told it to anyone, to include us, her parents. She was extremely hurt, confused, and ashamed. Somehow, she summed it up to being her fault. We saw the change immediately, but did not know what happened. She was withdrawn and easily frustrated. She literally changed from who we knew her to be to a totally different person. We didn't understand what she was going through, so we continued to pray and believe God would help us help her with what she was going through. She was thirteen at the time, so we thought it may have been a stage they go through.

The guy continued to torment her at school. She got to school the next week to hear people saying that she had sex with him. He discarded her and was walking with another girl the same day. There were others that turned away from her, and one girl wanted to fight her because she believed the lie and she was supposed to be his girlfriend at the time. It was devastating to her. We did not know about any of it because she held it in.

My daughter, Whitney, was so disturbed and distraught about what was happening to her. She was so young and fragile. She started being frustrated and very easily agitated at just about everything. Her beautiful smile changed. It was no longer there. She couldn't eat. She couldn't sleep. All of this went on and she had not told us anything. She said she thought we would be upset with her. Remember, somehow, the enemy convinced her that it was her fault. I had to correct her and tell her that's what the enemy wanted you to think so he could continue to torment you. She completely withdrew. She tried to cover it up. She tried to smile, but the hurt would always bleed through. I began to fast and pray. I asked her time and time again if anything had happened to her that she wanted to talk about, but she refused to tell me. She thought she was protecting us because his family was so well-known in the community. I knew in my heart that God was telling me something like that had happened, but when I asked and she refused to tell me, I would continue to pray and ask God to reveal what was wrong. I bought her things, but things could not fix the effects of what happened to her. I prayed with her and talked, but the enemy had convinced her that she was to blame. Finally, out of desperation, we sent her to a youth camp at a well-known place that was recommended by some church friends called The International House of Prayer (IHOP) in Kansas City, Missouri. That was where she got her breakthrough. They encouraged and taught them to fast and pray. They took them to the prayer room daily to encourage them to soak in the presence of God. She began to love his presence. It was a three-week long program that changed her life forever. She was attending one of the prayer conferences there, and one God-sent wonderful woman of God was moved by the power of God to go over to her during prayer and whisper what happened to her in her ear and began to pray for her healing. She then began to open up through the power and love of God and told the story to her. The woman, I'll call Debra, impressed upon Whitney that she must tell her parents and that it wasn't her fault. She then told us, which was one of the single most hurtful thing I have ever had to happen to me. I say that because it did not just affect Whitney, it affected the whole family. It affected us all in a deeply hurtful way. We were totally and completely devastated. She told us with shame and so much hurt in her eyes. She said she would cry every night in the shower. She was taught about forgiveness and she would pray and tell God that she forgave him. She said she prayed in the shower and cried out to God to help her.

Whitney developed a spirit of fear from this experience that took her approximately nine years to get free from. She went off to college, but she had to have friends everywhere she went. God showed me one night when she came home for the Christmas holidays, and I prayed with her about it. I told her that God said she was living in bondage to fear and he was ready to free her if she was willing to let it go. She said she knew it was God because she had started praying about it herself and someone at church spoke the same words the previous Sunday. Letting go of it was the key to her freedom. Trusting it in God's hands is what she had to do in order for him to heal her and take away the fear and pain.

When we got done praying, she spoke these words to me, "I'm free now, Mom, I know it!" What a sigh of relief it was. She began to feel lighter. She was a whole lot less agitated and edgy. I told her she was easier to get along with, and I knew she was free from it. So much of her life was tangled up in that one experience, but when she got free from that bondage of fear, she began to embrace life with a new outlook. She told me, "I see things differently now."

Whatever kind of bondage you find yourself in will steal your joy, peace, and that abundant life that's promised to us. I listened as she began to talk a little about her feelings. I saw her transform before my eyes. It was beautiful. She smiled and smiled all day long. She couldn't wait to go back and explain to her best friend what happened to her and that she was free, and she will never go back to that bondage. The hurt lifted and she just plain let it go, all of it. You see God wants to free you in such a way that you know the freedom is so much better than your present state so that you will not even consider going back to that bondage. True freedom refuses to be bound by anything. What you need to do is understand that God has given us power and authority over that bondage and has entrusted you to put it in its place and that's under your feet. Just get rid of it and live free. Whatever it may be, God is ready when you are.

Do not allow bondage to bind you, turn around and bind it. Don't let it bind you up any longer. Just bind up those circumstances and hindrances. Flip the switch on that bondage and bind it. You can then loose true freedom in Christ. Matthew 18:18 says, "Assuredly, I say to you, whatever you bind on earth will be bound in heaven, and whatever you loose on earth will be loosed in heaven." Now take authority over all of it and start binding up some things. Then loose what God has for you. Loose the blood of Jesus over all of it. Loose what God is putting in your spirit to have. Loose the Word of God over it all. He will bring it to pass in your life. Freedom is yours for the taking. Live free! Once you embrace freedom, oh, it's so sweet! I cannot begin to tell you how good it feels, but you can experience it for yourself, just as I have.

I had a habit of carrying around burdens to the point that I never had peace of mind. My mind was always going and thinking about what may or may not happen. My husband would tell me to stop analyzing everything. Stop thinking so much. He was so right. He really should have told me to stop worrying so much. I had to get to the point of trusting God totally. I had to believe he loved me. I began to pray about worrying. I kept hearing God say, "Trust me." I was reminded of Proverbs 3:5–6, "Trust in the Lord with all your heart, and lean not on your own understanding; in all your ways acknowledge Him and He shall direct your path." I had to stop relying on my own self thinking things through, being afraid of the what ifs and just simply trust him. Over and over again, I would speak out his word over myself and meditate on those scriptures. I would say a scripture every time the enemy tried to make me worry. I still have to continue to fight the urge to worry and thank God for the victory. God is so faithful. Even when we are not faithful, he continues to be faithful to his word. Just begin to thank him. Thank him for working it all out for you. Thank him for hearing and caring and acting on your behalf. Believe his word and thank him for his promises.

He led me to 1 Peter 5:7: "Casting all your care upon Him, for He cares for you." I started giving everything to God and thanking him for the victory and thanking him for being there for me to give it all to with no strings attached. You have to decide to let go and let God. That's not just a cliché. Although people say it often, we have to do it as often as we say it. Casting over and over again all the cares of our lives.

Praising God is another way to break free because you begin to focus on him and not on everything else. That is, if you are focusing on him and listening to the words as you sing them and not on the circumstances. Don't let the enemy rob you of the power of praise by making you just say the words while thinking on all your burdens. God told me one day to defocus and refocus, meaning to stop focusing on the issues while I was praising him and focus on him. Matthew 15:8-9a: "These people draw near to Me with their mouth, and honor Me with their lips, but their heart is far from Me. And in vain they worship Me." I was guilty of doing that until God showed me that scripture. From that point, I never let the enemy get away with making me focus on the wrong thing during worship. Never allow your praise and worship to be in vain. We have to continue to remind ourselves about this as we begin to worship. Don't let your mind wander off onto other things. Focus on the Father and stay focused on him. Don't let the enemy still your adoration to the Lord. The enemy wants you to be so preoccupied with issues that when you get to church, you are too overwhelmed with worry to worship. We were not created to worry. That's why worry and stress does so much harm to our bodies. We were created to worship. Worship frees us and takes away all heaviness. Begin to worship God with your whole heart, focused totally on him. Enter into his presence and see won't things change. Things will change and you will change. You will start to feel the weight lift off of you and God will empower you with his presence. He will captivate you and bathe you with the essence of him. He will show you how big He is and how He cares for you and will take all your burdens away from you. Just begin to worship him now. "Oh, worship Him in the beauty of His holiness, Tremble before Him, all the earth" (Psalm 96:9). You will become light as a feather. He will take everything that overwhelms you and give you rest. Exchange what you have for what he has for you. Let his presence overtake you. Believe me, you certainly will not regret it. He is the absolute best thing that ever happened to me. Yes, I do mean, happened to me because to know him is to experience him. Just writing these words makes me stop and meditate on his love.

> Come to Me, all you who labor and are heavy laden, and I will give you rest. Take My yoke upon you and learn from Me, for I am gentle and lowly in heart, and you will find rest for your souls. For My yoke is easy and My burden is light.
>
> Matthew 11:28–30

His presence is where we need to be and the enemy fights it. Let's get preoccupied with him so we won't have room for anything else to bombard our thinking. Bombard yourself with worship, not worry. Let your life be filled with worshiping him. Worship him daily. Thank him daily. Believe him daily.

As we continue on in him, he sheds his light upon us and gives us all the answers we need. We don't have to take on anything that loads us down. He wants to take those things from us. We have to begin to realize that God is ready, willing, and able to take on all we have to deal with. As we believe that and receive his help, we can trust him to do what it takes in his timing. Sometimes, our timing is off and we think his timing is off.

> Be anxious for nothing, but in everything by prayer and supplication, with thanksgiving, let your requests be made known to God; and the peace of God, which surpasses all understanding, will guard your hearts and minds through Christ Jesus
>
> Philippians 4:6–7

The word *anxious* there means "full of cares." The word *but* there means "on the contrary." So don't be full of cares, on the contrary in everything, with thanksgiving make your requests known to him. I love the amplified version of this scripture, which makes it so plain:

> Do not fret or have any anxiety about anything, but in every circumstance and in everything, by prayer and petition (definite requests), with thanksgiving, continue to make your wants known to God; and God's peace [shall be yours, that tranquil state of a soul assured of its salvation through Christ, and so fearing nothing from God and being content with its earthly lot of whatever sort that is, that peace] which transcends all understanding shall garrison and mount guard over your hearts and minds in Christ Jesus.

God's peace will garrison and mount guard over you. Wow, that is powerful. You see God's peace is not to be compared with any other. God's peace will surpass your understanding, set up a garrison, and mount guard over you. Man's peace is limited to circumstances or whether they want to give it to you or not. As we choose God's peace, it does so much more. His peace does exactly what we need it to do and more on top of that. It doesn't just relax you, it protects and guards you at the same time. That's the kind of pillow I want to lay on. Many times, when my heart and mind would get overwhelmed, God would place a picture in my spirit of me lying in his bosom. A place soft and calming with no one there, except him and I. My eyes closed, my heart and mind free to let go and relax in him. He is certainly a keeper. Countless times, I lay in his presence not wanting to move.

I'll take God's peace any day, time, or place. "Peace I leave with you, My peace I give to you; not as the world gives do I give to you. Let not your heart be troubled, neither let it be afraid" (John 14:27). I believe God for his peace in everything and in all places. His peace is sufficient. His peace will keep you in the right state of mind. I remember in the past when something negative would happen to me, I would get this piercing, burning feeling in my heart. It would burn with fear, intimidation, hurt, or whatever the enemy put in my heart to feel because of that negative situation. I would feel so down or let down. It would stifle my whole being and take my whole day, night, and week. I would worry and fret every day about it. Then God told me one day when it happened to me, "You see that feeling right there, that piercing, I never want you to feel that again. You don't have to let this happen to you. I'm touched with the feelings of your infirmities, I can feel that too, and I do not want you to feel that. Those types of feelings will weaken your heart. My word says, the joy of the Lord is your strength. Let my joy fill your heart instead. Let my joy be your strength through this. Rejoice in the Lord, always, again I say rejoice. If you are weak, that's okay, my strength is made perfect in your weakness. So I got this. Laugh, rejoice in the face of the enemy. Put a song in your heart instead." From that moment until now, when things happen that are negative, I let the joy of the Lord overtake me and I rejoice. I clap my hands and praise. Sometimes, I have to hold on to something not to worry, but I do it. I do whatever it takes not to let that feeling of pain overtake me again. I have not felt that piercing since then. God just starts to flood my spirit with scripture. He overshadows it all and allows me to make up my mind to believe him wholeheartedly. Believe God; he won't let you down. You can take that to the bank. If you can just center yourself in him when things happen, negative or positive, he will keep you stable. I'm convinced of that because there have been so many opportunities to panic, give up, or do the wrong thing out of impulse, but when I stop to hear from God, He shows me the right decision to make every time.

Experiencing him in times like that, strengthens your faith and trust in him. Really seek him, I promise you will find that he has always been there waiting on you to acknowledge him so he can be that present help his word says he will be.

We have to decide to trust him and let him come in so he can show us the truth about things that will truly lead us to be victorious in all our endeavors. He leads and guides us when we rely on him. Don't be led by your circumstances. Let God lead you through your circumstances. Completely slow down, take a deep breath, and call his name. Seek his face. He will show you the answer.

Seeking God requires diligence. It requires commitment. You have to really continue to pursue him. I don't mean he's hard to find. I mean, with all the distractions the enemy tries to put in your way, you have to have a made-up mind that you will not let the enemy stop you no matter what. He will use whoever and whatever he can to stop you from relentlessly pursuing God. That's why we have to be vigilant in our pursuit of the Father. It takes time to get to know God. If it takes time to get to know people and they are right here tangibly with us. It's going to take time to know him, and believe me, he is worth every second you put into seeking him.

God will start to confirm your time with him. You may be driving down the road and see a sign that he will use to remind you of something he showed you in his word. You may be in church and the pastor is speaking on the very thing you were studying in his word. You may be at the supermarket or the gym and someone may need the scripture you just went over during your study and prayer time. Circumstances can no longer bind you up when you rely on him. The enemy hates it when you don't let things weigh heavy on you. God starts to become your greatest influence, not people and their opinion.

BONDAGE TO UNFORGIVENESS, RESENTMENT, AND BITTERNESS

> Then came Peter to Him, and said, "Lord, how often shall my brother sin against me, and I forgive him?" Jesus said to Him, I do not say to you, up to seven times: but up to seventy times seven.

> Matthew 18:21-22

Please do not take this point lightly. If you do not forgive, you are literally blocking the flow of kingdom power in your life. I must repeat myself, it is imperative that you understand that if you do not forgive, you block the flow of kingdom power in your life. That means everything you are praying for or praying for God to do through you is held up or I should say clogged up by unforgiveness.

> And whenever you stand praying, if you have anything against anyone, forgive him, that your Father in

> heaven may also forgive you your trespasses. But if you do not forgive, neither will your Father in heaven forgive your trespasses.
>
> Mark 11:25–26

You are blocking your own prayers when you do not forgive. Lack of forgiveness blocks access to the kingdom and to its unlimited power. You were created for more than where you are, but unforgiveness is holding you down, holding you captive, and locking up all God has for you. This type of bondage is so subtle and tricky because you are doing it to yourself and you go around with a mask on trying to hide it, but it bleeds out in so many areas in our lives. Some we are not even aware of. That is the tricky part. You have masked it so well, you do not even realize it is what's holding you back, keeping you from your breakthrough, and keeping you from your destiny. Forgiveness is the key. Other sins can be present, and if your heart condemns you for some other sin, then you definitely will not have confidence toward God. But most often, it is a lack of forgiveness that comes between people and God. You may think that you cannot let it go. With God's help and a clear understanding of why you should, yes, you can let it go.

The first step to recovery from this bondage is admittance and recognition of your resentment. Could it be yourself or maybe even God himself? Some people are holding something against God. Maybe you feel he didn't act on your behalf about an issue you were dealing with. Some people are holding things against others. They may have hurt you or wronged you in some way. Some people are holding things against themselves. You may have messed up in the past and did things you regret. You are holding yourself captive. You have the key to freedom and that is forgiveness, use it. You may feel justified in your feelings of unforgiveness and that may very well be, from man's perspective, but as we explore God's perspective, you will see a vast difference in the two perspectives, God's versus man's. I elect to pursue and apprehend God's perspective.

You will not be forgiven of your own faults if you do not forgive. "For if you forgive men their trespasses, your heavenly Father will also forgive you. But if you do not forgive men their trespasses, neither will your Father forgive your trespasses" (Matthew 6:14–15). Your forgiveness from God himself is contingent upon you unconditionally forgiving others. I know you are thinking, "You mean to tell me, God won't forgive me if I don't forgive others?" No, I'm not telling you, Jesus himself is telling you. God is extremely concerned with the nature of our hearts as the aforementioned reasons indicated. You hold yourself prisoner when you don't forgive. You can choose to let it go for your own self-interest or you can feel justified in your unforgiveness and keep yourself prisoner to your choice to not forgive. We should forgive again and again, everybody, everywhere, and all the time. It is obvious that forgiveness is truly in my best interest. The enemy will always give us opportunity to hold on to things because he knows how it affects our lives. The enemy knows he can sit back and watch you destroy yourself and others around you if you do not forgive unconditionally.

Unforgiveness harbored in the heart of a believer is often the reason they have not received their breakthrough. It is like a clog in a drain that stops the flow of water going through the pipes. It hinders God from freely giving you what you desire. It makes you vulnerable to your own weaknesses because the enemy has something in your heart he can use to gain access into your life. This is one subject that I think God wants us to truly meditate on because he wants to flow through our lives without delay, but when we choose to hold on to things, he then has to wait until you decide to forgive in order that he will move on your behalf in that situation or any other thing you ask him to do in your life. One of the single most important things you should do in your life is to forgive and keep on forgiving. You will always have opportunity to hold grudges because you will always have haters or people that do things against you, but we must continue to keep a clean heart before our Father and forgive over and over again, even if it's the same person or same thing. This is not for you to keep putting yourself in a situation that someone can do whatever they want and repeatedly mistreat you, absolutely not. However, I am saying that repeated forgiveness in your heart has to take place. Jesus forgave, all the way to the cross. Let's not allow the enemy power over our blessings by harboring unforgiveness inside of us. Once forgiveness takes place, then healing can take place.

I often say we should forgive and love, forgive and love, forgive and love. To the point our hearts are prone to do it without delay. What if during the delay, there are blessings that we forfeit, which were assigned to be delivered to us during that time. Yes, even if that person does not ask for forgiveness for the simple fact that the outcome of your forgiveness will affect you, not that other person. Believe me, I know it's hard because of the hurt you feel or the anger, but just release it and all the emotional turmoil to God. Then he will take action on your behalf, if necessary. That other person is living life in freedom, but you, on the other hand, are held in bondage to your own choice to refuse to forgive. To a certain degree, by holding on to things, we are passively getting back at the people who hurt us and taking vengeance, but the problem with that is they aren't being affected by the unforgiveness, we are. Simply because we hold ourselves prisoner to resentment and bitterness toward whoever hurt us. Also, the word says in Romans 12:19, "Dearly beloved, avenge not yourselves, but rather give place unto wrath: Vengeance is mine; I will repay, says the Lord." Do not take what belongs to God. He says specifically here that vengeance belongs to him.

Cleanse yourself from that hidden sin of the heart and be cleansed from secret faults. Ask God for a pure heart. Ask him to forgive you for harboring unforgiveness and cleanse you from all unrighteous. Cleanse you to the point that your heart feels the urge to pray for them. That would weaken the power of darkness in your life and empower you to move into more blessings flowing in your own life. "Not returning evil for evil, or reviling for reviling: but on the contrary blessing; knowing that you were called to this, that you may inherit a blessing" (1 Peter 3:9).

Let's flip the switch on the enemy. Instead of holding on to unforgiveness, let's hold on to forgiveness. You see when you hold on to offense, it's like taking drugs. It makes you paranoid. Your thinking isn't as clear as it should be at times because you try to compare other things to that offense and it takes away from the true meaning of things. Always be ready to forgive instantly, redeem the time. Trust God with it. Think of it this way: if you are always ready to forgive, you won't give the enemy any room in your life, not for a moment. You take away his power over you. That way you will never be bound by unforgiveness. The moment someone does something to you forgive them in order to never be in a position that the enemy can clog the flow of kingdom power in your life and stop your blessings. I know you may be saying, that's hard to do, but as I remember this principle of kingdom power flowing through forgiveness, I can quickly ask God to help me forgive and give me a clean heart toward that person. Now we are doing this for ourselves so that we won't be held captive and imprisoned to unforgiveness. I'm believing God for too much to let any moment be wasted on unforgiveness. Let's allow forgiveness to captivate us. At the moment of offense, forgive. "This being so, I myself always strive to have a good conscience without offense toward God and Men" (Acts 24:16). As you have a desire to forgive instantly and ask God to help you with those hurt feelings, you can forgive even though you may still have some pain, it will soon disappear. God will come in and soothe you with the comfort of the Holy Spirit. I often think of laying in his arms as he strokes all the hurt away. I lay there as he comforts me and replenishes me. He delivers me with such love and compassion. He is well aware of what I am going through, and he longs to hold me close to relieve me of all pain. I love it. He loves me. He loves me. He loves you too. He desires to do it for you too. Will you allow his touch, his peace, his deliverance, his will in your life?

Let's take a look at Stephen. After being used mightily by God to speak to the people, he was falsely accused of blasphemy by a group of haters, oops, I mean a group that rose up against him. Let's read what God says about them.

> Then there arose some from what is called the Synagogue of the Freedmen (Cyrenians, Alexandrians, and those from Cilicia, and Asia), disputing with

> Stephen. And they were not able to resist the wisdom
> and the Spirit by which he spoke.
>
> Acts 6:9–10

The haters, I mean Freedmen, could not stand hearing the truth of God. They tried to dispute with him, but could not overpower him because he was filled with the Holy Spirit and the power of God was leading him. He was then brought before the council. "And all who sat in the council, looking steadfastly at him, saw his face as the face of an angel" (Acts 6:15). Stephen was in a place that he could still reflect God's glory even though he was being falsely accused. He did not waste time on unforgiveness. God's glory showed up on him without delay. He recognized that he had work to do and he spoke without delay.

Stephen then gave a powerful message before the council, which further angered the crowd.

> When they heard these things they were cut to the
> heart, and they gnashed at him with their teeth. But
> he, being full of the Holy Spirit, gazed into heaven
> and saw the glory of God, and Jesus standing at the
> right hand of God.
>
> Acts 7:54–55

He maintained a heart of forgiveness. Stephen didn't focus on the crowd, he focused on Jesus. If his heart was not pure, he would not have been able to see Jesus. "Blessed are the pure in heart, for they shall see God" (Matthew 5:8).

The people began to yell and run toward him to stone him. Can you imagine: they were like brute beasts, howling at him and running toward him with stones in their hands throwing them at him. What a sight that must have been. The most amazing part of this story is the fact that Stephen kept a pure heart toward them, which is evidenced by his response to their stoning him. "Then he knelt down and cried out with a loud voice, 'Lord, do not charge them with this sin,'" and when he had said this he fell asleep'" (Acts 6:60). Stephen not only kept a pure heart, but he forgave them in the process of them stoning him to death to the point where he took it to the highest measurement possible to do for your enemies, he prayed for them. God will comfort your heart through the forgiveness process. Stephen was still ministering to his accusers all the way to his death because he cried with a loud voice. To me, that meant he wanted them to know he forgave them and that the message of God was more important than what they were doing to him. He was interceding for them. What a powerful witness, they were able to hear him praying for them while they were stoning him to death. That was the last thing they heard from him, which was a prayer "for" them. I'm sure that stuck in the minds of his accusers as a powerful witness to the power of God. I can imagine some of them did not sleep well after that. I wonder if God didn't use that powerful witness to save some of them. As they gazed at him praying for them, did some of their hearts soften toward this man of God and realize this man was truly sent by God?

Let us forgive expediently the way Stephen did in order for God to purify our hearts, and we will not be bound by unforgiveness. Kingdom power will continue to flow in our lives. "But I say to you who hear: Love your enemies, do good to those who hate you" (Luke 6:27). Stephen was full of the Holy Spirit and power. Let's not be full of resentment and bitterness. Let's instead be full of the divine love of God. As we love people with God's love in us, we can take the beatings we often have to take. God's love is strong enough to take it.

When we ask God to forgive us for our sins at the point of salvation, he immediately forgives us. As much as he hates sin, he forgives us of all present, past, and get this, future sins. Bless the name of the Lord! That is absolutely beautiful! Our heavenly Father, Abba, is granting us grace to mess up and ask for forgiveness even before we commit the sin. "For You, Lord, are ready to forgive, And abundant in mercy to all those who call upon You" (Psalms 86:5). I simply refuse to hold offense. I refuse to hold a grudge. It is totally unprofitable for me and for the kingdom of God. No one ever gained anything by holding a grudge. Inevitably, someone always gets hurt. Hurting people hurt people. They were hurting long before they hurt you. Choose to let it go so that the Comforter can come in and heal you. That way when you see that person again, you can be free to love them in spite of all offense. You see that's how you can confuse and diffuse the enemy. What a powerful concept. Truly, it takes God to come up with stuff. Let's be honest, there is no way man could have come up with this concept of forgiveness. "Therefore if your enemy is hungry, feed him; if he thirst, give him drink: for in so doing you will heap coals of fire on his head. Be not overcome by evil, but overcome evil with good" (Romans 12:20–21). Those coals are going to go in and melt or soften their heart toward you and God can get some good out of it. Evil begets evil, but good begets good. Who knows, God may even have that person or people, who were once your enemy, to turn around and bless you. I've known people who become friends for life by using this concept, God's way.

God is very clear concerning forgiveness in scripture. I have chosen to abide by the word of God no matter what. I want to be so blessed that I am in a position to bless others. I endeavor to get everything God has for me and by that same token, I endeavor to do everything God tells me to do. "But he who looks into the perfect law of liberty and continues in it, and is not a forgetful hearer but a doer of the work, this one will be blessed in what he does" (James 1:25). Yes, I definitely mess up from time to time, no doubt about that, but I thank God for his grace to repent and plead the blood and ask for forgiveness with the assurance that I am forgiven. Oh, what sweet grace. The grace of God does not keep record, it just gives me the room I need to get it right. The blood of Jesus took care of it all for us.

Just think of Jesus on the cross. "Then Jesus said, Father forgive them, for they do not know what they do" (Luke 23:34). Jesus forgave them even as they spat on him going up Calvary with the cross on his back. Some people don't even realize they hurt you. Some people do realize it, but because they are hurting, their feelings are severed to you and what they have done to you. Their hurt masks your pain. Please do not allow someone else's hardened heart to harden yours. Allow God to give you a heart that is ready to forgive. He wants us to get to the place in him that we want what he wants. He desires for his will to supersede our will. Sometimes, we've been hurt so bad, we don't want to forgive. That is where that relationship with God comes in. As we get closer to him, we begin to really know him and we want what he wants. That does not mean it will be easy, but we will long to please him to the point we want to be obedient to his word.

The Holy Spirit has a way of giving you strong urges on the inside that is hard to ignore.

> I will give you a new heart and put a new spirit within you; I will take the heart of stone out of your flesh and give you a heart of flesh. I will put My Spirit within you and cause you to walk in My statutes, and you will keep My judgments and do them.
>
> Ezekiel 36:26–27

That scripture goes on to describe the blessings that will overtake us when we obey. I don't know about you, but I just cannot arbitrarily pass up the blessings of God that comes along with a pure heart.

When I think of Joseph, a pure heart before the Lord comes to mind. First of all, Joseph had to have a pretty good relationship with God and an attentive ear to his voice for him to have been able to interpret dreams at such a young age. That young man was so in tune with God that he was able to interpret his own dreams and other people's dreams as well. His heart is what I want to focus on here because he forgave his brothers without them even asking. It was evidenced in his ability to win favor with Potiphar who made him overseer over his house. He also granted Joseph favor by sparing his life after he was accused by Potiphar's wife of trying to sleep with her. Joseph was sent to prison by Potiphar instead of being put to death, which was the normal punishment for what he had been accused of by Potiphar's wife. Even in prison, he was favored. I can tell you, it was not because of harboring unforgiveness in his heart.

> But the Lord was with Joseph, and showed him mercy, and gave him favor in the sight of the keeper of the prison. And the keeper of the prison committed to Joseph's hand all the prisoners that were in prison; and whatsoever they did there, he was the doer of it. "The keeper of the prison did not look into anything

> that was under Joseph's authority, because the Lord
> was with him; and whatever he did, the Lord made
> it prosper.

> Genesis 39:21–23

Whatever Joseph touched, God made to prosper. You do not gain all that favor with a hard and impure heart. Joseph kept his heart clean by forgiving his brothers and moving on and kingdom power kept flowing in his life, clog free. Joseph continued in his faith in God and did his will no matter where he found himself. Life kept dealing him bad hands, but he played them to the glory of God and God granted him favor and delivered him out of it all. God restored Joseph with more than he had before. He gained the ultimate favor from Pharaoh himself by interpreting his dream correctly. The blessings of God remained with Joseph throughout his life in and out of prison because of his forgiveness. Joseph got promoted by God because of his forgiving heart. Joseph was then able to use his gift inside the prison and his gift is what God used to free him and bring him before great men. "A man's gift will make room for him and bring him before great men" (Proverbs 18:16). Joseph redeemed the time and did not allow unforgiveness to stop what God could do for him, even in prison. He trusted God and continued doing what God would have him to do in every situation. There is no time to be spent on unforgiveness. It is a complete waste of valuable time and effort. It would have stifled what God had in store for Joseph. Keep your heart clean before the Lord and he will bless you, no matter the circumstances. God gave Joseph authority even in prison.

> So the advice was good in the eyes of Pharaoh and in the eyes of all his servants. And Pharaoh said to his servants, "Can we find such a one as this, a man in whom is the Spirit of God?" Then Pharaoh said to Joseph, "Inasmuch as God has shown you all this, there is no one as discerning and wise as you. You shall be over my house, and all my people shall be ruled according to your word; only in regard to the throne will I be greater than you. And Pharaoh said to Joseph, "See I have set you over all the land of Egypt." Then Pharaoh took his signet ring off his hand and put it on Joseph's hand; and he clothed him in garments of fine linen and put a gold chain around his neck. And he had him ride in the second chariot which he had; and the cried out before him, Bow the knee!
>
> Genesis 41:37–43

His blessings didn't stop there. It gets even better because Pharaoh gave Joseph the daughter of a priest to marry. They had two sons, Joseph expressed his heart through the names of his sons.

> And Joseph were born two sons before the years of famine came, whom Asenath, the daughter of Poti-Pherah' priest of On, bore to him. Joseph called the

name of the firstborn Manasseh: "For God has made me forget all my toil and all my father's house." And the name of the second he called Ephraim: "For God has caused me to be fruitful in the land of my affliction.

Genesis 41:50–52

That is what it means to flow in kingdom power. Streams of blessings were given to Joseph. God and everyone else around Joseph knew his heart was pure concerning his hardship. Bless the name of the Lord! God caused Joseph's sons to be born before the famine even occurred. God kept Joseph's heart in such a pure state that he was able to give him all the desires of his heart. "But He knows the way that I take; When He has tested me, I shall come forth as gold" (Job 23:10). Just think of Joseph's witness in the midst of his suffering. Joseph continued to pray and stay close to God. The Lord heard his prayers. God knew Joseph's pain and suffering. He knows your pain as well. He is touched with the feelings of our infirmities. This means he literally feels your pain. Joseph never let them forget who his God was. They knew who Joseph served and they accepted his conviction to serve the only true and living God. Pharaoh never tried to make him bow down to their many gods because God had shown himself as Almighty through the life and witness of Joseph. God lavished Joseph with such powerful favor. Joseph's witness in the midst of his suffering obviously pleased God.

"For what credit is it if, when you are beaten for your faults, you take it patiently? But when you do good and suffer, if you take it patiently, this is commendable before God" (1 Peter 2:20). The grace of God kept Joseph, and he reigned in life because of God's grace. This affliction was used by God to buffet Joseph before he received what God had promised him through his dreams. God showed Joseph what he was going to become when he was a child, but there was a process that had to take place inside of Joseph first.

> And lest I should be exalted above measure by the abundance of the revelations, a thorn in the flesh was given to me, a messenger of satan to buffet me, lest I be exalted above measure. Concerning this thing I pleaded with the Lord three times that it might depart from me. And He said to me, "My grace is sufficient for you, for My strength is made perfect in weakness." Therefore most gladly I will rather boast in my infirmities, that the power of Christ may rest upon me.
>
> 2 Corinthians 12:9

Let's explore what Joseph's life would have been like if he had not forgiven and continued to believe and trust God. Indulge me as I attempt to dictate to you an alternate ending to Joseph's life. Can you imagine if Joseph had not forgiven them and got thrown into prison? He probably would have been still held bound, down in the dungeon of the prison telling his sob story. Telling his "woe is me" story to the other prisoners and giving grand pity parties. He would have had lots of company because misery loves company. He would have had a captive audience to include many more years in prison rehearsing his sob story as he told them over and over again. What a poor witness that would have been. God would not have gotten any glory out of that. No, Joseph had a choice to nurse his wounds that definitely would not have healed or forgive and move forward allowing his God to reign in his life no matter what. He certainly would not have gotten the favor of God on his life. I remember during one of my grand pity parties, I mean it was so dramatic. I sobbed and wept and blew my nose and sobbed and wept and blew my nose some more. I looked in the mirror as I sobbed and blew my nose. I wonder why is it that you look in the mirror when you cry. I said, "God, help me, I'm hurting." I distinctly remember hearing God say, "I do not attend pity parties, I inhabit the praises of my people." All the weeping and sobbing stopped in an instant. I'm so happy it was just God and myself at that particular pity party because I would have been so embarrassed if anyone else heard him say that to me. "In everything give thanks; for this is the will of God in Christ Jesus for you" (1 Thessalonians 5:18). I heard that scripture in my spirit, and I began thanking him and praising him. I felt the peace of God overwhelm me as I praised him and thanked him. I was filled with so much faith as I started lifting him up and not my problem.

The favor of God set Joseph up in such a way that he was put in command second to the king in a foreign land. He wasn't even Egyptian and Pharaoh knew it. God wants to set you free and set you up. What marvelous kingdom power that flowed in the life of Joseph. He got great position and possession. Pharaoh decked Joseph out with gold and one of the finest chariots. God granted Joseph the desires of his heart. The Bible goes on to say that Pharaoh also gave him a wife and Joseph had two sons. God not only gave him what he needed, which was his freedom, but God gave him the desires of his heart. I believe there is a difference between the blessing of a need being met and the desires of your heart being granted. You see you can still get blessed, but not with the deep desires of your heart. Joseph got both. What a blessed life God wants to lavish on us. He desires to give us the desires of our hearts and blessings.

The story goes on to the point of Joseph meeting up with his brothers in need and he had the power to meet their need. There was a famine in the land and his brothers went to Joseph to buy grain, not knowing it was Joseph. Let's check out the actions of Joseph towards his brothers when they came to him for help during the time of famine.

> When Joseph saw Benjamin with them, he said to the steward of his house, "Take these men to my home, and slaughter an animal and make ready; for these men will dine with me at noon.
>
> Genesis 43:16

When God sets a table before you in the presence of your enemy, will you have the heart Joseph had and share it or will you rub it in their face and turn away? Joseph certainly had that choice, but he chose to bless his brothers instead. Joseph was able to see the hand of God over his life during his time of suffering from the hands of his brothers. He was only able to see the hand of God because he forgave them and he didn't blame God for his circumstances either. He continued to keep God first in his life and pray for God to move on his present circumstances.

> And God sent me before you to preserve a posterity for you in the earth, and to save your lives by a great deliverance. "So now it was not you who sent me here, but God; and He has made me a father to Pharaoh, and lord of all his house, and a ruler throughout all the land of Egypt.
>
> Genesis 45:7–8

There would be no way Joseph could have come to that conclusion on his own without God revealing that truth to him. His heart was open to listening to God and yielding to God's will. I believe with that God took the pain away as well. I know that's what happens to me when God tells me to do something good for those who have hurt me. Joseph would have continued blaming his brothers and definitely would have still been in a stuck place wondering why his God hasn't blessed him to get free when all along his "woe is me" mentality was blocking kingdom power. There would be no forgiveness in his heart only self-pity. No he chose the high road and rose above unforgiveness and his circumstances to receive what God had in store for him. Joseph saved his brothers lives contrary to them trying to destroy his. Joseph loved his brothers and wanted to reconcile with them despite what they had done to him. Now that is a heart that is pure and forgiving.

> Therefore, if your enemy is hungry, feed him; If he is thirsty, give him a drink; For so doing you will heap coals of fire on his head." Do not be overcome by evil, but overcome evil with good.

> Romans 12:20

Joseph kept the word of God and received more than he could ask or think. We have to see this as an example of true forgiveness in its finest form. He not only forgave, but he took it a step further and gave them what the needed to include saving their lives.

You may say, "God I just can't forgive that person." Change that around and speak the word over yourself. "I can do all things through Christ who strengthens you" (Philippians 4:13). I say to you, yes you can. You can do it. After you forgive, you will feel the peace of God embrace you and overtake you.

I don't know about you, but I would rather be overtaken by the peace of God than by the bondage of unforgiveness.

As we begin to draw close to God, he begins the process of renewal in our minds and hearts. He starts to show us more of himself. The way he loves on us is like no other. The sweetness of his presence gives us a sense of belonging and tranquility. He helps you to believe his word as you experience him shower you with the love and grace he has for us. You are right where you need to be in mind, body, and spirit in his presence. You never want to leave him. Get there; it's wonderful. The peace you will feel is matchless. Peace will begin to lead all your decisions. I remember when I first experienced true peace. It melted on me like butter, and I soaked it up like toast. It was refreshing. It was invigorating. I was packed with the blessed assurance of a Savior that loves me dearly and is aware completely of me and my circumstances.

"And be kind to one another, tenderhearted, forgiving one another, even as God in Christ forgave you" (Ephesians 4:32). There are countless benefits to a forgiving heart. Forgiveness brings freedom. Forgiveness brings light. Forgiveness cleanses the heart. Forgiveness sets us up for blessings. Forgiveness brings growth and maturity. Forgiveness exposes the hidden things of the heart so God can come in and work on us. Forgiveness shows our obedience and love for God. Forgiveness shows our love for ourselves. Forgiveness clears our vision. If you are in the same place or worse off now than you were a year ago, maybe you need to do some inventory on your heart to see what is in there that's blocking the flow of blessings and kingdom power in your life. Singing, dancing, shouting, and speaking in tongues are not enough if unforgiveness is lingering in your heart toward someone. Believe with me that in the face of adversity, in the face of evil, in the face of my enemies, in the face of persecution, and in the face of backbiters, I forgive, I love, and I am free. Declare it, believe it, and receive it in Jesus's name.

There is also a point that has to be made of you asking for forgiveness yourself. Is there anything that you have done to someone that you need to ask their forgiveness? That is also a blessing and kingdom power blocker. Will you admit that there are things you may have done to people that you are not proud of? Have you been the one on the giving end of the hurt? If so, God has something He wants you to do. He wants you to ask for forgiveness. "Confess your trespasses to one another, and pray for one another, that you may be healed" (James 5:16a). If you know you have hurt someone and you know God's heart concerning forgiveness, then by the grace of God you need to ask them to forgive you. You can do it with the help of the Lord. Do not allow pride to hinder your blessings. The grace of God will enable you to do it. He will lead and guide you. Ask him to show you who, when, and how. Depend totally on him, and he will take you through the whole process. If someone had done some wrong toward you, I'm sure you would like for them to ask for forgiveness. "And just as you want men to do to you, you also do to them likewise" (Luke 6:31). I know this is a big pill to swallow, but God will help you get it down. You never know how that will help to free your heart and the heart of the person you hurt. They may not receive your apology, but that is not up to you to decide. It is imperative that you ask for forgiveness so that as you begin to go forward in Christ, the enemy will not have anything to hold over your head. Let the love of God overtake you. He will work through you to accomplish his will. You see, he is looking for a willing vessel, but we have to be willing. You may think it's a small thing, but not so. Not in God's eyes. They are responsible to forgive after you ask with a pure heart. They may even get belligerent with you because of the unforgiveness lodged on the inside of them. Maybe they have allowed their heart to be hardened toward you. It is going to take courage to do it, but do it to the glory of God no matter how they respond. "If it is possible, as much as depends on you, live peaceably with all men" (Romans 12:18). You will have a good conscience before God. That could very well be the point of your breakthrough. Humble yourself to do the will of God, and he will meet you with strength and ability and he will lift you up. Do not allow pride to grip your heart and stifle your growth and maturity in him. "A man's pride will bring him low: but the humble in spirit will retain honor" (Proverbs 29:23). Your blessings are hanging in the balance until you decide to let God rule in your heart. Who knows you may win a soul in the process. You can begin to witness to them about what God has done in your life and how you are no longer that person anymore. You have a new heart, and your new heart asks for their forgiveness. As you begin to tell them about the goodness of God in your life and how he opened your eyes and gave you a new life, that person may see a glimmer of light and decide to give their life to Christ as well. God can do anything. I know of testimonials that when someone had to go to another person and ask for forgiveness, that soul got saved. Some gave their lives to Christ that very instance and some later. The glory of God will show up in you as you depend on him through it. You will have a clear conscience and be able to flow in your gifts freely.

> Therefore, if you bring your gift to the altar and there remember that your brother has something against you, "leave your gift there before the altar, and go your way. First be reconciled to your brother, and then come and offer your gift.
>
> Matthew 5:23–24

Whatever the case may be whether or not it is received, after you do it, you are free. I had to bring this point out because so many people ignore their own deeds. They are so focused on what someone else has done to them that what they have done to others conveniently slips their mind. I had to be reminded myself of things I have done. God is reminding you today to do it. I have done things to others that God has told me to go back and apologize to them. After I humbled myself and was obedient, the glory of God shined through me. He graced me through it. My heart was at peace afterward, and I could move forward without something hanging over my head. Yes, I felt awkward and it was so uncomfortable, but I stepped out of the comfort of pride and humbled myself in order to be obedient to God. I remember many times having to go to my husband and asking for his forgiveness. I did not want to do it at all, but it wasn't about what I wanted. It was about what God wanted. I have to admit that I messed it up sometimes and had to go and pray all over again. God told me one time, "Why are you asking me for forgiveness again, I have already forgiven you now, go back to him and get it right this time." Now, that was awkward, and I decided not to have to go back and get it right again. The Holy Spirit will quicken you to do it. Do not ignore it. I've done it at work so many times. I've done it at home with my husband and my kids and whoever else I may have hurt. God wants to get that out of the way so he can bless you. Could that be the one thing that is holding you back? Will you continue to allow the enemy to rule in your heart or will you give in to the power of God working in your heart? By doing the latter, you will allow God's power to flow through you mightily. Oh, we pray, "God flow through me, let your Holy Spirit flow through me." He is trying to get this done so he can. This is what it's going to take to unplug the clog and open the flow. Bless the name of the Lord! Cleansing will take place and blessings will flow.

God told Jacob to return to the land of his family. I can imagine Jacob may have been thinking about what he did to his brother Esau by stealing his birthright. Jacob then sent messengers to Esau before he got to him to offer him animals and servants to make peace with him because Esau had vowed to kill him. "I have sent to tell my lord, that I may find favor in your sight" (Genesis 32:5). The messengers reported to him that Esau was coming to meet him with four hundred men. Fear struck Jacob and he began to devise a plan. The fact that he included God in that plan was the only reason he was blessed.

> Then Jacob said," O God of my father Abraham and God of my father Isaac, the Lord who said to me, 'Return to your country and to your family, and I will deal well with you' "Deliver me, I pray, from the hand of my brother, from the hand of Esau; for I fear him, lest he come and attack me and the mother with the children. For you said, 'I will surely treat you well, and make your descendants as the sand of the sea, which cannot be numbered for multitude.
>
> Genesis 32:9, 11–12

Jacob trusted God. He was a changed man. He no longer had the same heart. God had cleansed his heart and humbled him. He humbled himself before his brother Esau who he had wronged and God touched the heart of Esau.

> Then he crossed over before them and bowed himself
> to the ground seven times, until he came to his brother.
> But Esau ran to meet him, and embraced him, and fell
> on his neck and kissed him, and they wept.
>
> Genesis 33:3–4

God touched Esau's heart as well to forgive Jacob and Esau was blessed also. Esau was blessed with plenty before he even got to Jacob. He didn't want to take what Jacob was offering him to bless him because he was so blessed already, but Jacob insisted and Esau took the blessing and obtained more. God later renamed Jacob, Israel. His sons were the twelve tribes of Israel. Can you imagine what would have taken place if Jacob had not humbled himself and been obedient to the Lord. "God resists the proud, But gives grace to the humble" (1 Peter 5:5b). God knew the twelve tribes of Israel were at stake. There is something greater for you. God has so much more planned for you. Do not allow a simple apology to keep it from you. God has an astonishing array of blessings just waiting for you to inherit.

Part 2: It's in him, we live and move and have our being.

FUNCTIONING BONDAGE

Functioning bondage is when you are able to maintain your outside life such as holding a job and other relationships, but inside you are disheveled and full of pain. This is where denial is prevalent because there is no outside evidence. You could even fool yourself into thinking that you are fine, but inside every now and then, something hits you and you cannot explain your behavior. You get stuck, but cannot explain why. Things just start to go downhill and you feel like you can't do anything about it. Do not accept a life of living in bondage. Many people have accepted bondage to the degree they are functioning in it. Let me explain this by saying take the mask off and trust God. One way people live and function in bondage is hiding what they are going through. Do not be in a state of denial. Don't allow yourself to get so accustomed to bondage that it is becomes comfortable. It becomes a way of life and you think it's okay to have the things in your life that binds you. The Lord shows you every now and then that you can be free, but you choose to stay in a state that is most familiar. Even though you do not like it and you know it is not the will of God, you continue to function in life in a place of acceptance. After all, it would be so hard to change the way things have been for so long. You would have to do new things that are unfamiliar and it is a bit scary because you may fail. You don't think it would yield the results promised. There are so many people that are afraid of what they are not familiar with. You don't have to fall in that number. As a matter of fact, after reading this book, I declare that you will begin to see things differently through the eyes of God and step out on the promises of God. They are for all of us and not just a few. Grab hold of them and never let them go. Apply his Word to your life and see won't you see clearer and have the faith to accomplish what he has so graciously made available to you. Admit where you are and believe God to break you out of it. You can do it. I have done it and many others. Won't you join us? Believe me, it's spectacular.

The person that is in bondage to another person/group will keep them in mind at all times. Everything you do has to line up with what they think. You are always within their reach. It is hard to tell the difference between them and God because you run to them for their opinion on everything. Then you consult God and tell him what you plan on doing. That is backward and certainly not the will of God. He wants you dependent on him, not them. When you measure who

NO MORE BONDAGE |

you would rather impress the most, God loses. They win because you are afraid of losing them. Really, it comes down to the relationship with them you don't want to lose. Your relationship with them is more important to you than your relationship with God. Your vision gets blurry and you begin to see through their eyes.

You see the people of Israel were functioning as they worked and toiled in the fields, but they were miserable in the process. They were burdened down in the process. They were not able to do anything they wanted to do because of being under the rule of Pharaoh who pressed them down with slavery. They had the potential to be a great people as evidenced by their being able to multiply the way they did even though they were held down by Pharaoh, but they were unaware of the power of God that was at their disposal until Moses came along and rescued them by the power of the Almighty God. God demonstrated to them and the Egyptians that he was their Lord, their resident owner and he was not going to allow them to be held in bondage any longer.

We are "the redeemed." We have been bought with a price. We have been purchased with the powerful blood of Jesus Christ. We have the right to all sorts of power with that blood. We need to receive it, believe it, and appropriate it. He has given us the power over our past, present, and future circumstances through the blood of Jesus. There is nothing that has the power or authority over the blood of Jesus. We overcome by the blood of the Lamb and the word of our testimony. "And they overcame him by the blood of the Lamb and the word of their testimony" (Revelations 12:11a). We have encountered some things in our past that have held us captive for far too long. We can take the authority that the blood of Jesus gives us and take all power from the enemy. We have to realize the love God has for us, and he also wants to see us free from those things so he can give us the abundant life he has in store for us.

Since we have been purchased, we are God's property. He has the final say-so about what goes in and out of us, and he has given us authority as well through his powerful blood. That being established, the enemy has been trespassing on God's property for far too long and getting away with it. You can kick him out by the power of the Holy Spirit every time he tries. Trust God pass the enemy's trespasses.

When you are in bondage to circumstances, life, or issues, you take on everything as if everything is all right, when all the while, you are miserable. You can't see your way out. You try and try, but to no avail. Circumstances get heavier and heavier. You look on the outside as if all is well, but on the inside, you are bound. You wear a mask that is automatic. At home, it comes off. Outside of home, right at the door, it automatically sticks to your face, smile, and all. You still carry all the burdens inside. You go, but it's always there in the back of your mind reminding you of its power over you.

Reminding you of the heaviness it lays on you. You have planted good seed on the inside of you, but it just does not come to its full bloom because it's hindered by this bondage that you are under. When Jesus talks about the parable of the sower, you find he explains this clearly:

> And that which fell among thorns are they which, when they have heard, go forth, and are choked with cares and riches and pleasures of this life, and bring no fruit to perfection.
>
> Luke 8:14

Scattered seed among thorns or the cares of life choke out the seed. At some point, the thorns or issues eat at your seed and it cannot come to maturity. Every time you try to push forward, the bondage shows up and locks you down. You cannot get ahead because you are held down by this heavy load. It stifles your growth, kingdom power, and restricts and hinders your blessings. Even your blessings get trampled on by this bondage, but you still try to hide it and move along in life without being effective.

The bondage of unforgiveness is one of the most systematically debilitating because it blocks kingdom power in your life. Many people have decided that they are not going to forgive and have accepted that thing on the inside of them that controls their life. They function with hidden unforgiveness. You can smile outside, but the mask is really painted on well. Your life continues on and you can even forget about it until the enemy wants to pull your string and remind you of the hurt so you can be miserable and relive those same feelings all over again. The mask, however, is automatic. You can hide the unwillingness to forgive, after all, you feel justified based on what happened to you. You freshly smile every day even though beneath it all is that thing you haven't forgiven. Sometimes, you even forget about it, but because the enemy hasn't, he brings it back to your remembrance as if it just happened. You may wonder why you haven't gotten your breakthrough. This is probably why. You are holding on to something that really has turned and is holding you.

The signs of functioning bondage that are so prevalent with so many people is having no peace, being easily agitated and frustrated, having depressive moments or spans of time especially when you are alone. The smiles go away because you don't have to pretend when you are alone. Your heart bleeds because of the unforgiveness. You are easily offended and have a heightened sense of the negativity in everything you see. You have to begin to apply the blood of Jesus over yourself. The blood of Jesus will free you and give you all the answers you need to release you and kingdom power in your life. It will wash all of that stuff out of you so that you will have true smiles and effective fruit that will grow to its full potential.

After hearing a sermon my husband preached on forgiveness, it was as if I had heard it for the first time. I realized I was carrying unforgiveness toward so many people that I had to make a list and verbally call them out to God and tell him that I forgive them and I let it all go. I ended up on the floor in tears. I began to search the scriptures that were given during the sermon so that I could really get a clear understanding of what God wanted out of me. The freedom I felt planted a real smile on my face. It gave me a sense of security and peace. I could think of those people again and not have resentment hidden inside my heart. God told me that once I forgave them, I was released and I could through away the key I locked myself up with and throw it away because as long as I remembered His take on forgiveness and was obedient I would never be bound again with unforgiveness. What freedom I felt. I stopped comparing everything someone did to me to what had happened to me by the hands of others and let things go easier. My smile now is true freedom from the inside. I love God for helping me free myself. I flow in my gifts like never before. I am secure in my gifts like never before. I believe in God as a deliverer like never before. He has delivered me from myself, and I will not let me hold me ever again. That may sound crazy, but that is basically it, me holding me. Although it took several steps, the process was worth every effort I put forth. I have to continue to forgive because the enemy will not stop using people to do things, but my perspective has changed drastically and I look at things differently now. I know without a doubt that I would not be where I am today without having done the things God told me to do concerning forgiveness.

I simply trusted God. "Trust in the Lord with all your heart and lean not unto you own understanding in all your ways acknowledge Him and He will direct your path" (Proverbs 3:5–6). I studied that scripture until it connected with my spirit man. I told God I give him my whole heart and I know I can trust him with it. There is not room for resentment when you give God your whole heart because He won't allow it. He will nudge you and let you know that you are moving toward that and tell you not to have that in your heart. I asked him to create in me a clean heart and renew a right spirit in me and He did. I continue to pray that so my heart can stay pleasing to Him through all my circumstances as I recognize the potential dangers of something impure entering in to hinder or make it unclean. I smile for real all the time now, and it is absolutely wonderful. My heart is light as a feather because when you hold on to unforgiveness, when others do things to you, all of it is lodged inside your heart and creates a thick clog. Once I forgave, all that other stuff had nothing to hold on to. It was gone and I said good-bye, see ya! So much evil can get lodged inside of you that you just cannot imagine. My heart began to be free flowing and so did kingdom power, love, blessings, and gifts of the Spirit.

I had to forgive myself for my mistakes. I had to forgive others that hurt me, and I had to forgive God for thinking he let those things happen to me. I know all of that stuff hurt, but I believe with all my heart I would not be who I am today, had I not gone through them. It is an ongoing process and as things happen, be quick to forgive. Remember, give God your whole heart and he will convict you to keep it clean and pure before him that he may give you the desires of your heart.

I really gave it over to him so he could show me what to do with it. That is exactly what will catapult you into an arena of dependency on him. The security in knowing he is on your side and taking care of your cares is so comforting. "Casting all your care upon Him, for He cares for you" (1 Peter 5:7). Aren't we so blessed to have the ability to pitch everything we are going through to him and leave it all with him. We don't have to worry about it and go back and check to see if he is doing the right thing. We can be assured that God is well able and willing to work all things out for our good. Take the time to ponder on how wonderful it is to be able to do that. The Lord cares for us and is waiting on the opportunity to be that ever present help.

This may be one of the hardest things to do. Leaving your cares with him and not picking them back up and doing what you think is best. Learn to depend on him by doing that. Learn that he is going to work it all out for your good by experiencing him when you leave it with him. I had to learn that God didn't need my help. I had to learn that God expected me to come to him and not try to handle things on my own just to mess things up worse. I had to get to the point and am still learning to rest in him after I lay it all on the altar. I am still learning that his ways are higher than my ways, and I don't see things at his viewpoint until he reveals it to me. Resting in him does not mean being lazy. It means not worrying about the situation and relying on him to work things out for your good. God has a perfect plan and a divine strategy. Ask him to reveal to you his divine strategy on what is your next step and you will see him reveal his way, which is far better than our own way. You may not get in detail everything he has in store, but the next step will definitely be revealed. God knows the details will probably scare us and make us want to turn back so He lovingly and strategically takes us through a series of steps. He loves us so much he does not want to burden us with the details. He wants to see faith steps.

Step by step, he will show you the best way to stay free from everything that has held you captive and will restore all the enemy took from you during the time you were in bondage. Restoration in every dimension of human experience is at the heart of the Gospel of Jesus Christ. The Blood of Jesus has covered our sins. This includes present, past, and future sins.

We can rest in the truth that God wants to restore us more than we want to be restored that's why he is longsuffering with us. He truly longs to restore us. Restoration is interwoven all throughout the scriptures and should be the primary goal of every ministry. God is well aware of our shortcomings, our mistakes, and our sins, but his love abides with us and he is always ready to be reconciled with us and restore us. I want to say here that God's restoration is so much better than before. According to the dictionary, "to restore" means to "bring back to a former or original condition." This is not the case with God's restoration. To be restored according to God's plan of restoration is always increased, multiplied, or improved so your latter state is better than your former state. "So I will restore to you the years that the swarming locust has eaten, the crawling locust, the consuming locust, and the chewing locust, My great army which I sent among you" (Joel 2:25). You will surely be better than before. God intends to make sure of it. Just follow his lead, he will show you the way and make your path straight before him. He will make things clear to you. I can definitely say, "I can see clearly now the bondage is gone."

When God restored Job after all the turmoil he had been through, he gave him twice what he had lost and blessed him more than in the beginning. As God begins to free you, at first, it will be hard and may look insurmountable, but he will provide you with the strength and the ability to do what it takes on your part to break free and stay free. Leaning and depending on the Father is imperative as you break free from all sorts of bondage. You not only want to break free, but you want everything the enemy stole from you and more. Trust him through the pain and agony of letting go. The blood of Jesus has bought your freedom, take it and live free forever. Never to be overtake by any form of bondage again. "Now the Lord blessed the latter days of Job more than his beginning" (Job 42:12a). Job had more after God restored him than before. God restores us and makes us better than before.

Job forgave and prayed for his friends even though they spoke against him. That shows his willingness to submit himself to God and move out of the way so that God could move on his behalf. That is what we need to do as we forgive. We need to move out of God's way and let him bless us as we forgive others. There is a distinct connection between our forgiveness and our blessings. We have to begin to realize the way we think about things must line up with the Word of God. God's way is the right way. When he restores us, he completely washes away all residues from us. We can move away from past hurts and never even look, sound, or smell like the dirt we have been involved. That's the God we serve. He does a complete work in us. I am so amazed at the love he has for us. I cannot stop thinking about his love. In so many ways, he magnifies his love for us. He is absolutely wonderful in all his ways. I just want to stop and say here, "I love you too,

Lord." He is so compassionate with us and our circumstances. He is more acquainted with our feelings than we are. He knows just how much we can bear. "And the Lord restored Job's losses when he prayed for his friends. Indeed the Lord gave Job twice as much as He had before" (Job 42:10).

There is no need to live in bondage to anything. We are God's property and should not be bound to anything. Once we figure that out, it will set you free to be who God called you to be. When he gets our attention and teaches us who we really are we will be amazed at the power and authority we have to live in true righteousness and freedom. No foe can withstand God's power. We will have our spiritual eyes and ears open to all that may come our way. Not to be overly sensitive, but spiritually alert and vigilant not to be vulnerable to any form of bondage. When you truly find freedom you will be amazed at the things you miss while locked up. Life passes you by and you are stuck on lock down to things you have power over. Do not ignore freedom. Our freedom was not free, it cost Jesus too much, his very life. He went to hell and back to give us this freedom and we should do whatever it takes to stay free and appreciate his unfailing, unconditional, never-ending love.

God will free you everywhere you are bound. Then he wants to use you to free others. You become more sensitive to others that are bound and your heart goes out to them because you know the feeling and you don't want anyone else to live that way. I made a pact with myself to never live bound again to anything or anyone. My freedom cost Jesus too much.

> Stand fast therefore in the liberty by which Christ has made us free, and do not be entangled again with a yoke of bondage.
>
> Galatians 5:1